# Had Gadya

# Had Gadya
## A Passover Song

Paintings by
## Seymour Chwast

Afterword by
Rabbi Michael Strassfeld

A Deborah Brodie Book
Roaring Brook Press
Brookfield, Connecticut

This book is dedicated to peace.

A note on the pronunciation: The "H" in *Had* is pronounced like the "ch" in *Bach*.

A note on the art: Seymour Chwast created outline drawings in pen and ink, which he scanned and printed as a blue outline on heavyweight paper. These then served as a guide for the paintings, which he did in acrylics.

Illustrations copyright © 2005 by Seymour Chwast
Afterword copyright © 2005 by Michael Strassfield

A Deborah Brodie Book
Published by Roaring Brook Press
A Division of Holtzbrinck Publishing Holdings Limited Partnership
2 Old New Milford Road, Brookfield, Connecticut 06804

Distributed in Canada by H.B. Fenn and Company Ltd.

Library of Congress Cataloging-in-Publication Data
Had gadya. English.
Had gadya = One little goat : a Passover song / with paintings bySeymour Chwast ;
afterword by Michael Strassfeld.—1st ed.
    p.    cm.
"A Deborah Brodie book."
Summary: An illustrated, bilingual version of this cumulative folk song that is sung at the end
of the Passover Seder. Includes a background note on the history and symbolism of the song.
1. Had gadya—Juvenile literature. 2. Seder—Liturgy—Texts—Juvenile literature.
3. Judaism—Liturgy—Texts—Juvenile literature. [1. Passover—Songs and music.
2. Jews—Music. 3. Folksongs, Aramaic. 4. Folksongs, English. 5. Aramaic language materials—Bilingual.]
I. Title: One little goat. II. Chwast, Seymour, ill. III. Strassfeld, Michael. IV. Title.
BM670.H28C4813 2004
296.4'5371—dc22        2003017831

ISBN 1-59643-033-8
10 9 8 7 6 5 4 3 2 1

Roaring Brook Press books are available for special promotions and premiums.
For details contact: Director of Special Markets, Holtzbrinck Publishers.

Book design by Seymour Chwast
Printed in the United States of America

First edition

An only goat,
   an only goat
My father bought
   for two zuzim.
*Had gadya,*
   *had gadya.*

Then came
the cat
And ate
the goat.
*Had gadya,*
*had gadya.*

Then came
the dog
And bit
the cat.
*Had gadya,
had gadya.*

Then came
the stick
And beat
the dog.
*Had gadya,*
*had gadya.*

Then came
the fire
And burned
the stick.
*Had gadya,
had gadya.*

Then came
   the water
And quenched
   the fire.
*Had gadya,
   had gadya.*

Then came
the butcher
And killed
the ox.
*Had gadya,
had gadya.*

Then came
  the Angel of Death
And slew
  the butcher.
*Had gadya,*
  *had gadya.*

Then came God
And destroyed
the Angel of
Death.
*Had gadya,*
*had gadya.*

Have fun singing this song – whether you are using this English transliteration or the Aramaic original. You can take turns acting out and making the noises that identify each character or object. For example, bleat each time the goat (*gadya*) is mentioned. Meow for the cat (*shoonra*), bark for the dog (*khalba*), bang for the stick (*hutra*), sizzle for the fire (*noora*), make "glub glub" sounds for the water (*maya*), low for the ox (*tora*). You'll need to get creative for the butcher (*shohet*), the Angel of Death (*malakh ha-mavet*) and God (*ha-kadosh barukh hu*). The illustrations in this book may give you more ideas.

Had gadya, had gadya.
Deezvon abba beetray zuzay.
Had gadya, had gadya.

V'ata shoonra v'akhal legadya, deezvon abba beetray zuzay.
Had gadya, had gadya.

V'ata khalba v'nashakh leshoonra, d'akhal legadya,
Deezvon abba beetray zuzay.
Had gadya, had gadya.

V'ata hutra v'heeka lekhalba, d'nashakh leshoonra, d'akhal legadya,
Deezvon abba beetray zuzay.
Had gadya, had gadya.

V'ata noora v'saraf lehutra, d'heeka lekhalba, d'nashakh leshoonra,
d'akhal legadya, deezvon abba beetray zuzay.
Had gadya, had gadya.

V'ata maya v'khava lenoora, d'saraf lehutra, d'heeka lekhalba,
d'nashakh leshoonra, d'akhal legadya, deezvon abba beetray zuzay.
Had gadya, had gadya.

V'ata tora v'shata lemaya, d'khava lenoora, d'saraf lehutra, d'heeka
lekhalba, d'nashakh leshoonra, d'akhal legadya, deezvon abba
beetray zuzay.
Had gadya, had gadya.

V'ata ha-shohet v'shahat letora, d'shata lemaya, d'khava lenoora,
d'saraf lehutra, d'heeka lekhalba, d'nashakh leshoonra, d'akhal
legadya, deezvon abba beetray zuzay.
Had gadya, had gadya.

V'ata malakh hamavet v'shahat leshohet, d'shahat letora, d'shata
lemaya, d'khava lenoora, d'saraf lehutra, d'heeka lekhalba, d'nashakh
leshoonra, d'akhal legadya, deezvon abba beetray zuzay.
Had gadya, had gadya.

V'ata hakadosh barukh hoo v'shahat lemalakh hamavet,
d'shahat leshohet, d'shahat letora, d'shata lemaya, d'khava lenoora,
d'saraf lehutra, d'heeka lekhalba, d'nashakh leshoonra,
d'akhal legadya, deezvon abba beetray zuzay.
Had gadya, had gadya.

# Had Gadya

Traditional
Arranged by Jerry Silverman

# About *Had Gadya*

Though hardly able to pick our heads off the Seder table from all the wine and talk (to say nothing about the food), the singing of the folk song *Had Gadya* always seems to give us a second wind just as the Passover Seder ends. Its simple words and melody belie a deeper and perhaps darker meaning that is often obscured by the lateness of the hour. Designed to provoke the curiosity of children (which is one of the main purposes of the entire evening), the series of folk songs at the end of the Seder, of which *Had Gadya* is by far the best known, are late additions to the Haggadah text, added sometime around the fifteenth century. The folk quality of these songs is reflected in the numerous versions that exist in the vernacular languages of the Jewish Diaspora. At our Seder, my father would sing one of these tunes in both its Yiddish and its Ukrainian versions.

*Had Gadya* is called a chain folk song because its cumulative style tells a tale. Up until its last stanzas, there is nothing obviously Jewish or religious about the song. Perhaps the unknown author took a general folk song and added a Jewish ending. The way it is sung and its placement at the end of the evening has given *Had Gadya* a light and fun nature. Yet some commentators on the Haggadah have interpreted the song in a more serious manner. The most common view is that it is a metaphoric telling of the story of the Jewish people, which is represented by the goat (*gadya*). The stanzas that follow employ animals like the cat and the dog, as well as objects like a stick and water, to symbolize the various enemies of the Jewish people. Each of these "empires" falls, disappearing into the dust of history. The triumph of God at the end of the song represents the triumph of the Jewish people, which has persevered despite all the centuries of persecution. In this way, *Had Gadya* echoes the earlier line from the Haggadah text: In every generation, our enemies arise against us but the Holy One saves us from them. *Had Gadya* becomes another expression of the larger theme of the Haggadah – that the story of oppression and liberation is our ongoing story. From this perspective, the song is a hopeful expression of the inevitable triumph of good in the world.

This understanding provokes many contemporary Jews. The noted writer Elie Wiesel wrote: "I loved this naïve little song…[but] I rebelled against the resignation it implied. Why does God always act too late? Why didn't God get rid of the Angel of Death before he even committed his first murder?" Chava Alberstam, one of Israel's foremost contemporary singer-songwriters, uses the traditional text of *Had Gadya* and then asks: "I have asked only four questions, but tonight I have one more question. How long will this cycle of horror continue? Persecutor and persecuted, beater and battered.…I already was a dove, I used to be a deer, today I don't know who I am.…Our father bought a goat for two zuzim, again we begin from the beginning."

Our version of *Had Gadya* can be understood in two ways. The first is that this remains a charming little folktale. The characters are set in some timeless shtetl—an Eastern European village that seems both old and contemporary at the same time. The tale unfolds amidst the family and community's preparing for the Seder night. The stick becomes the wood that feeds the fire that bakes the matzah. The preparation for Passover itself is part of this chain song, for all things are connected to what comes before and help to create what follows.

This points to the deeper meaning that unfolds here. There is a cycle of life that begins and grows and finally comes to an end. One generation will follow another. All things will pass from this earth. And yet, all things continue even if in another form. Seymour Chwast, in the two final images of the book, brings back the goat and the father, as though they had never left. Our story ends with the entire family and many of the characters dancing together, as though to suggest that there will come a time when the cycle will end not in death but in the death of death. God represents the hope that someday this story and every story will end with the words: and they all lived happily ever after.

*Rabbi Michael Strassfeld*

וְאָתָא הַקָּדוֹשׁ בָּרוּךְ הוּא      דְּשָׂרַף לְחוּטְרָא,

וְשָׁחַט לְמַלְאַךְ הַמָּוֶת,      דְּהִכָּה לְכַלְבָּא,

דְּשָׁחַט לְשׁוֹחֵט,      דְּנָשַׁךְ לְשׁוּנְרָא,

דְּשָׁחַט לְתוֹרָא,      דְּאָכַל לְגַדְיָא.

דְּשָׁתָה לְמַיָּא,      דְּזַבֵּן אַבָּא בִּתְרֵי זוּזֵי,

דְּכָבָה לְנוּרָא,      חַד גַּדְיָא חַד גַּדְיָא.